The Ultimate Guide to Cryptocurrency Investment:
A comprehensive Handbook for American Investors
LD Brock

Table of Contents:

- Ripple (XRP)
- Litecoin (LTC)
- Other notable cryptocurrencies

7. How to Invest in Cryptocurrencies
- Choosing a cryptocurrency exchange
- Setting up a digital wallet
- Strategies for buying and selling cryptocurrencies

8. Secure Investment Practices
- Importance of secure storage
- Best practices for securing your crypto assets
- Avoiding common scams and pitfalls

9. Resources for American Investors
- Recommended cryptocurrency exchanges
- Trusted sources for market analysis and research
- Regulatory bodies and legal resources

10. Conclusion and Next Steps
- Recap of key points
- Actionable steps for getting started with cryptocurrency investment
- Future outlook for the cryptocurrency market

Chapter 1: Introduction to Cryptocurrencies

Cryptocurrencies have emerged as a revolutionary form of digital currency, transforming the way we perceive and interact with traditional finance. In this chapter, we will delve into the fundamentals of cryptocurrencies, explore their historical roots, and discuss the compelling reasons why investors are increasingly drawn to this innovative asset class.

What are Cryptocurrencies?

At its core, a cryptocurrency is a form of digital or virtual currency that utilizes cryptography for secure transactions and operates on decentralized networks based on blockchain technology. Unlike traditional fiat currencies issued by governments and central banks, cryptocurrencies are decentralized and typically rely on a distributed ledger technology known as blockchain to record and verify transactions.

The concept of cryptocurrencies originated with the creation of Bitcoin in 2009 by an anonymous individual or group using the pseudonym Satoshi Nakamoto. Bitcoin introduced the groundbreaking concept of a peer-to-peer electronic cash system, allowing individuals to conduct transactions directly without the need for intermediaries such as banks or financial institutions.

Since the inception of Bitcoin, thousands of alternative cryptocurrencies, commonly referred to as altcoins, have been developed, each with its unique features, use cases, and underlying technologies. Examples of popular cryptocurrencies include Ethereum, Ripple, Litecoin, and Cardano, among many others.

Cryptocurrencies operate on decentralized networks, meaning that they are not controlled or regulated by any single authority or institution. Instead, transactions are verified and recorded on a distributed ledger known as the blockchain, which is maintained by a network of nodes or computers spread across the globe. This decentralized architecture ensures transparency, immutability, and censorship resistance, making cryptocurrencies inherently resilient to censorship and tampering.

Brief History of Cryptocurrencies

The history of cryptocurrencies dates back to the late 20th century, with the concept of digital cash being explored by various researchers and cypherpunks. However, it wasn't until the introduction of Bitcoin in 2009 that cryptocurrencies gained mainstream attention and adoption.

Bitcoin's creation marked the beginning of a new era in digital finance, offering a decentralized alternative to traditional fiat currencies and financial systems. Over the years, Bitcoin has experienced exponential growth in value, market capitalization, and adoption, paving the way for the proliferation of alternative cryptocurrencies and blockchain-based projects.

In the years following Bitcoin's launch, a wave of innovation swept through the cryptocurrency space, leading to the development of alternative cryptocurrencies, blockchain platforms, decentralized applications (DApps), and smart contract protocols. Ethereum, launched in 2015 by Vitalik Buterin and a team of developers, introduced the concept of programmable money, enabling developers to build decentralized applications and execute smart contracts on its blockchain.

Since then, the cryptocurrency ecosystem has continued to evolve rapidly, with new projects and technologies emerging to address various challenges and opportunities in areas such as decentralized finance (DeFi), non-fungible tokens (NFTs), and blockchain interoperability.

Why Invest in Cryptocurrencies?

The allure of cryptocurrencies as an investment asset stems from several compelling factors:

1. Potential for High Returns: Cryptocurrencies have exhibited significant volatility and price appreciation, offering the potential for high returns for investors who can navigate the market effectively.

2. Diversification: Cryptocurrencies provide an opportunity for portfolio diversification, allowing investors to hedge against traditional asset classes such as stocks, bonds, and real estate.

3. Blockchain Technology: Blockchain technology, the underlying innovation behind cryptocurrencies, has the potential to disrupt various industries and transform business processes, making cryptocurrencies attractive to investors seeking exposure to this disruptive technology.

4. Inflation Hedge: Some investors view cryptocurrencies, particularly Bitcoin, as a hedge against inflation and currency devaluation, given their limited supply and deflationary issuance model.

5. Accessibility: Cryptocurrencies offer accessibility to financial services for individuals in underserved or unbanked regions, democratizing access to capital, savings, and investments.

6. Decentralization: The decentralized nature of cryptocurrencies offers resilience against censorship, government intervention, and financial repression, appealing to proponents of individual sovereignty and economic freedom.

7. Global Reach: Cryptocurrencies operate on a global scale, enabling frictionless cross-border transactions and facilitating financial inclusion for individuals in regions with limited access to traditional banking services.

8. Technological Innovation: Cryptocurrencies are at the forefront of technological innovation, driving advancements in areas such as blockchain scalability, privacy, and interoperability. Investors are attracted to the potential for groundbreaking innovations and paradigm shifts in finance and technology.

9. Community and Ecosystem: Cryptocurrencies have vibrant and active communities of developers, enthusiasts, and entrepreneurs driving innovation and adoption. Investors are drawn to the collaborative and open-source nature of cryptocurrency projects, which fosters creativity, experimentation, and peer-to-peer collaboration.

10. Speculative Opportunities: The cryptocurrency market offers speculative opportunities for investors to capitalize on short-term price movements, trading strategies, and market trends. While speculative investing carries higher risks, it also presents opportunities for significant gains for investors with a high tolerance for risk.

In conclusion, cryptocurrencies represent a transformative force in the global financial landscape, offering a decentralized alternative to traditional fiat currencies and financial systems. With their innovative technology, potential for high returns, and disruptive capabilities, cryptocurrencies have captured the imagination of investors worldwide and continue to reshape the future of finance in profound ways.

Chapter 2: Understanding the Crypto Market

In this chapter, we embark on a comprehensive exploration of the intricate dynamics of the cryptocurrency market. We'll delve into its volatility, market cycles, trends, and the myriad of risks associated with investing in cryptocurrencies.

Market Dynamics and Volatility

The cryptocurrency market is a dynamic and volatile ecosystem, characterized by rapid price movements and market fluctuations. Unlike traditional financial markets, where prices are influenced by factors such as economic indicators, geopolitical events, and central bank policies, the cryptocurrency market operates 24/7 and is driven primarily by supply and demand dynamics, investor sentiment, technological developments, and regulatory news.

Volatility is a defining feature of the cryptocurrency market, with prices often experiencing significant fluctuations over short periods. This volatility can be attributed to several factors:

1. Limited Market Liquidity: The cryptocurrency market is relatively small compared to traditional financial markets, which can lead to pronounced price swings in response to large buy or sell orders. Illiquidity in certain markets or trading pairs can exacerbate volatility and contribute to unpredictable price movements.

2. Speculative Trading: Many participants in the cryptocurrency market engage in speculative trading, seeking short-term profits from price fluctuations. Speculative activity can amplify market volatility, as traders react to news, rumors, and market sentiment, leading to exaggerated price movements.

3. Market Sentiment: Investor sentiment plays a crucial role in driving cryptocurrency prices, with market participants often reacting emotionally to

news events, regulatory developments, or technological advancements. Positive news or announcements can trigger buying frenzies and price rallies, while negative news can lead to panic selling and price crashes.

4. Technological Factors: Technical developments and innovations within the cryptocurrency ecosystem can impact market sentiment and price volatility. Updates to blockchain protocols, security vulnerabilities, network upgrades, or changes in mining algorithms can influence investor confidence and market dynamics.

Despite its inherent volatility, the cryptocurrency market also presents opportunities for traders and investors to profit from price fluctuations. Traders employ various strategies such as day trading, swing trading, arbitrage, and trend following to capitalize on short-term market movements. However, it is essential to approach trading with caution and implement risk management strategies to mitigate potential losses.

Market Cycles and Trends

The cryptocurrency market operates in cycles, characterized by alternating periods of bull and bear markets. These market cycles are influenced by a combination of factors, including investor psychology, market sentiment, technological advancements, regulatory developments, and macroeconomic trends.

1. Bull Markets: Bull markets are periods of sustained optimism and rising prices, characterized by widespread enthusiasm and bullish sentiment among investors. During bull markets, cryptocurrency prices experience significant appreciation, driven by factors such as increased adoption, positive news flow, institutional investment, and speculative buying. Bull markets are often accompanied by rising trading volumes, FOMO (fear of missing out) among investors, and media hype.

2. Bear Markets: Bear markets, on the other hand, are periods of prolonged price declines and pessimism, characterized by widespread fear and bearish sentiment among investors. During bear markets, cryptocurrency prices undergo significant corrections or downtrends, triggered by factors such as regulatory uncertainty, security breaches, market manipulation, or macroeconomic headwinds. Bear markets can test investors' resolve and patience, leading to panic selling and capitulation.

3. Market Trends: In addition to market cycles, cryptocurrencies exhibit long-term trends based on fundamental factors such as adoption, technological

innovation, regulatory clarity, and macroeconomic trends. Identifying and analyzing these trends can help investors identify investment opportunities and position themselves for long-term growth and success in the cryptocurrency market.

Understanding market cycles and trends is essential for investors to make informed decisions and navigate the cryptocurrency market effectively. While it is challenging to predict the timing and duration of market cycles, recognizing key indicators and patterns can help investors identify potential turning points and adjust their investment strategies accordingly.

Risks Associated with Crypto Investments

Investing in cryptocurrencies carries various risks, including:

1. Price Volatility: The volatile nature of the cryptocurrency market can result in significant price fluctuations and potential losses for investors. Prices can experience rapid swings in response to news events, market sentiment, or trading activity, making it challenging to predict and manage investment risk.

2. Regulatory Risks: Regulatory uncertainty and government intervention can impact the legality, trading, and adoption of cryptocurrencies, leading to uncertainty and market volatility. Changes in regulatory policies or enforcement actions by regulatory authorities can affect investor confidence and market dynamics.

3. Security Risks: Cryptocurrency exchanges, wallets, and protocols are susceptible to security breaches, hacks, and theft, posing risks to investors' funds and personal information. Security vulnerabilities, bugs, or exploits in cryptocurrency software or infrastructure can result in financial losses and reputational damage for investors and service providers.

4. Market Manipulation: The unregulated nature of the cryptocurrency market makes it susceptible to market manipulation, fraudulent schemes, and insider trading. Pump-and-dump schemes, wash trading, spoofing, and other forms of market manipulation can artificially inflate or depress prices, leading to losses for unsuspecting investors.

5. Technological Risks: Vulnerabilities in cryptocurrency protocols, smart contracts, and blockchain networks can result in security vulnerabilities, bugs, or network disruptions, affecting the value and usability of cryptocurrencies. Software bugs, coding errors, or consensus failures can lead to chain splits,

network forks, or other technical issues that impact investor confidence and market stability.

6. Liquidity Risks: Some cryptocurrencies may suffer from low liquidity, making it challenging to buy or sell large amounts of assets without affecting market prices. Low liquidity can lead to price slippage, increased trading costs, and difficulty exiting positions, particularly in illiquid markets or trading pairs.

Despite these risks, many investors are attracted to cryptocurrencies due to their potential for high returns, portfolio diversification benefits, and exposure to innovative technologies. However, it is essential for investors to conduct thorough research, exercise caution, and employ risk management strategies before investing in cryptocurrencies.

In conclusion, understanding the dynamics, volatility, cycles, trends, and risks associated with the cryptocurrency market is essential for investors looking to navigate this fast-paced and evolving asset class. By staying informed, adopting a long-term perspective, and implementing risk management strategies, investors can capitalize on the opportunities while mitigating the risks of investing in cryptocurrencies.

Chapter 3: Legal and Tax Considerations

In this chapter, we delve into the intricate legal and tax landscape surrounding cryptocurrencies, crucial for American investors navigating this burgeoning asset class. Understanding the legal status of cryptocurrencies, taxation rules, and reporting requirements is paramount for complying with regulatory obligations and minimizing tax liabilities effectively.

Legal Status of Cryptocurrencies in the US

The legal framework surrounding cryptocurrencies in the United States is multifaceted and continues to evolve as regulators grapple with the complexities of this nascent asset class. At the federal level, cryptocurrencies are not recognized as legal tender but are treated as property by the Internal Revenue Service (IRS) for tax purposes. This classification means that cryptocurrency transactions, including buying, selling, or trading, are subject to capital gains tax, akin to other investment assets such as stocks or real estate.

While federal regulation directly addressing cryptocurrencies remains limited, various regulatory agencies hold oversight authority over specific aspects of the cryptocurrency market. For instance, the Securities and Exchange Commission (SEC) regulates initial coin offerings (ICOs) and considers certain cryptocurrencies to be securities subject to securities laws and regulations. Additionally, the Commodity Futures Trading Commission (CFTC) regulates cryptocurrency derivatives and futures contracts.

On a state level, individual states have adopted varying approaches to regulating cryptocurrencies and blockchain technology. Some states have embraced blockchain innovation by enacting favorable legislation or establishing regulatory sandboxes to foster innovation and investment. Others have imposed restrictions or licensing requirements on cryptocurrency-related businesses to address concerns regarding consumer protection, investor security, and financial stability.

Despite ongoing regulatory efforts, the legal landscape surrounding cryptocurrencies in the US remains fragmented and subject to interpretation. Clarity and consistency in regulatory guidance are crucial to fostering innovation and investment in the cryptocurrency ecosystem while protecting consumers and investors from potential risks.

Taxation of Cryptocurrency Investments

Taxation of cryptocurrency investments is governed by the tax laws and regulations enforced by the IRS. In 2014, the IRS issued guidance stating that virtual currencies, including cryptocurrencies, are treated as property for federal tax purposes. Consequently, capital gains tax applies to cryptocurrency transactions, with taxes levied on the difference between the purchase and selling price of a cryptocurrency when sold or exchanged.

The tax treatment of cryptocurrency transactions varies depending on several factors, including the duration for which a cryptocurrency is held and the nature of the transaction. Cryptocurrencies held for over a year before being sold or exchanged qualify for long-term capital gains tax rates, which are typically lower than short-term capital gains tax rates applicable to assets held for a year or less.

In addition to paying taxes on cryptocurrency transactions, investors are required to report their cryptocurrency transactions accurately on their tax returns. This includes maintaining detailed records of transactions, such as dates, amounts, and valuations in US dollars, to ensure compliance with IRS regulations.

Reporting Requirements for Crypto Transactions

In addition to paying taxes on cryptocurrency transactions, American investors must adhere to specific reporting requirements set forth by the IRS. Taxpayers engaging in cryptocurrency transactions are obligated to report these transactions on their annual tax returns, which involves:

1. Form 8949: Taxpayers are required to report capital gains and losses from cryptocurrency transactions on Form 8949, which is attached to Schedule D of their individual tax return (Form 1040).

2. Schedule 1: Taxpayers must also indicate on Schedule 1 of their tax return whether they have engaged in buying, selling, or exchanging virtual currencies during the tax year.

3. FATCA Reporting: Taxpayers holding cryptocurrency in foreign accounts may have additional reporting obligations under the Foreign Account Tax Compliance Act (FATCA).

Failure to accurately report cryptocurrency transactions or comply with reporting requirements may result in penalties, fines, or other enforcement actions by the IRS.

Navigating the legal and tax landscape surrounding cryptocurrencies can be intricate and challenging for American investors. It is imperative for investors to stay abreast of regulatory developments, adhere to tax laws and reporting requirements, and seek professional advice when necessary to ensure compliance and mitigate tax liabilities effectively.

By comprehending the legal status of cryptocurrencies, taxation rules, and reporting obligations, investors can make informed decisions and navigate the complexities of the cryptocurrency market with confidence.

Chapter 4: Assessing Investment Risks

The advent of cryptocurrency has revolutionized the financial landscape, offering unprecedented opportunities for wealth generation, democratizing access to global markets, and challenging traditional notions of currency and investment. For American investors, the allure of digital currencies lies not only in their potential for substantial returns but also in the novel dynamics they introduce to the portfolio diversification process. However, with great opportunity comes significant risk, and navigating the volatile waters of cryptocurrency investment requires a nuanced understanding of the unique challenges and pitfalls that lie beneath the surface.

This chapter delves deeply into the multifaceted nature of investment risks associated with cryptocurrencies, shedding light on the critical factors that American investors must consider to safeguard their investments. The volatile and unpredictable nature of the crypto market, coupled with the complexities of inflation, regulatory landscapes, and security concerns, presents a unique set of challenges. Understanding these risks is not just about preserving capital; it's about making informed decisions that align with one's investment goals, risk tolerance, and the ever-changing regulatory and economic environment.

Market Risk

Market risk, also known as systematic risk, is the possibility of experiencing losses due to factors that affect the entire market or a significant portion of it. In the realm of cryptocurrency, this type of risk is particularly acute due to the high volatility inherent in these markets. Cryptocurrencies can experience wide price swings in response to events such as regulatory announcements, technological breakthroughs, market sentiment shifts, and global economic developments. These fluctuations can be far more pronounced than those seen in more traditional financial markets, making cryptocurrencies a potentially high-reward but also high-risk investment.

The underlying cause of market risk in cryptocurrency is multifaceted. Primarily, it stems from the speculative nature of these assets. Unlike traditional investments, which may be underpinned by tangible assets or predictable cash flows, the value of cryptocurrencies is largely driven by supply and demand dynamics fueled by speculation. This can lead to rapid increases in value, followed by sudden and severe downturns. Additionally, the relatively young and untested nature of many blockchain technologies adds an element of uncertainty, which can further exacerbate market volatility.

Mitigating market risk in a cryptocurrency portfolio necessitates a strategic approach. Diversification is a fundamental principle, wherein investors spread their investments across a variety of assets to reduce exposure to the risk of any single investment's poor performance. In the context of cryptocurrency, this might mean holding a mix of different cryptocurrencies, including both established coins like Bitcoin and Ethereum and smaller, emerging tokens. However, true diversification also involves spreading investments beyond cryptocurrencies into other asset classes, such as stocks, bonds, and real estate, which may behave differently under the same market conditions, further reducing overall portfolio risk.

Another effective strategy for mitigating market risk is adopting a long-term investment horizon. Cryptocurrency markets can be particularly turbulent over short periods, but investors who are able to hold their investments through the ups and downs may see more stable returns over time. This approach requires patience and a strong belief in the long-term potential of cryptocurrency as an asset class. Additionally, staying informed about market trends and developments can enable investors to make more educated decisions, potentially avoiding the worst impacts of market downturns and capitalizing on opportunities as they arise.

Inflation Risk

Inflation risk refers to the erosion of purchasing power over time as prices for goods and services increase, diminishing the real value of money. For investors, the concern lies in the potential for their investments to not keep pace with inflation, leading to a decrease in the real value of their portfolio. This risk is particularly relevant in the context of traditional fiat currencies, where central banks can print more money, leading to inflation. However, in the cryptocurrency market, the dynamics of inflation risk are uniquely different due to the decentralized nature and often fixed supply of many digital currencies.

Cryptocurrencies like Bitcoin have introduced a novel approach to combating inflation. With a capped supply of 21 million coins, Bitcoin was designed to be deflationary, meaning its supply cannot be increased at will, in stark contrast to fiat currencies. This scarcity is a key factor that many believe will protect its long-term value against inflation. However, the relationship between cryptocurrencies and inflation is complex. While certain cryptocurrencies are designed to be immune to the inflationary pressures that affect fiat currencies, their value is not solely determined by these mechanics but also by market demand, technological developments, and broader economic factors.

To understand the impact of inflation on investments, it's helpful to look at historical data. For instance, the U.S. has experienced varying inflation rates from 1929 to 2023, with significant spikes observed during certain periods. The Great Depression marked a period of deflation, with prices falling dramatically. However, post-World War II, the U.S. saw inflation rates increase, peaking in the 1970s and early 1980s, with annual rates occasionally reaching into double digits. More recently, inflation has been relatively low, with the Federal Reserve targeting a 2% rate. However, the COVID-19 pandemic and subsequent economic policies have led to a resurgence in inflationary pressures, highlighting the persistent risk inflation poses to investors.

Mitigating inflation risk in a cryptocurrency portfolio involves several strategies. Firstly, diversification across asset classes that historically have performed well during high inflation periods can provide a hedge. Real assets, such as real estate and commodities, tend to maintain their value as prices rise. Similarly, investing in cryptocurrencies that have a fixed supply or deflationary mechanisms, like Bitcoin, can offer protection against the decreasing purchasing power of fiat currencies.

Another strategy involves the allocation to inflation-protected securities, such as Treasury Inflation-Protected Securities (TIPS) in the United States, which adjust the principal value of the bond to reflect inflation rates, thus preserving the real value of the investment. While this approach is more traditional and outside the direct realm of cryptocurrencies, it highlights the importance of a well-rounded portfolio that can withstand various economic conditions.

Lastly, staying informed about economic indicators and trends can help investors anticipate inflationary pressures and adjust their portfolios accordingly. For example, monitoring central bank policies, employment data, and consumer price index movements can provide early warning signs of inflation. This proactive approach allows investors to make strategic adjustments to their investment mix, potentially moving into assets more resistant to inflation before its impacts are fully realized in the market.

Regulatory Risk

Regulatory risk refers to the uncertainty and potential financial loss that investors face due to changes in laws and regulations governing the cryptocurrency market. This type of risk is particularly pertinent to the crypto industry, which operates at the intersection of technology, finance, and legal frameworks that vary significantly across jurisdictions. The decentralized and borderless nature of cryptocurrencies poses a challenge for regulators and policymakers, leading to a dynamic and sometimes unpredictable regulatory environment. For investors, this means that a regulatory announcement or legal change in a major market can have immediate and profound effects on the global value and accessibility of cryptocurrencies.

Since the inception of cryptocurrencies, there has been a significant evolution in how they are viewed and regulated by authorities worldwide. In the early days, there was a notable lack of regulation, which contributed to the wild west image of the crypto market, with issues like the Mt. Gox hack in 2014 highlighting the need for regulatory oversight. Since then, several countries have taken steps to define and regulate cryptocurrencies, each taking a unique approach. For example, in 2017, Japan recognized Bitcoin as a legal method of payment, bolstering the market. Conversely, in 2018, China cracked down on cryptocurrency exchanges and initial coin offerings (ICOs), which had a dampening effect on the market. In the United States, the Securities and Exchange Commission (SEC) has been increasingly active in issuing guidance and taking enforcement actions against certain aspects of the crypto industry, influencing market behavior and investor sentiment.

Mitigating regulatory risk involves several strategies. First and foremost, diversification can help. Just as spreading investments across different asset classes can protect against market volatility, diversifying geographically and across different cryptocurrencies can reduce the impact of adverse regulatory actions in any single jurisdiction or against any single cryptocurrency. Furthermore, staying informed about regulatory trends and potential changes is crucial. Investors should closely monitor news and announcements from key regulatory bodies, such as the SEC in the United States, the Financial Conduct Authority (FCA) in the UK, and others relevant to the jurisdictions in which they invest.

Engaging with legal and financial advisors who specialize in cryptocurrency regulations can also provide a buffer against regulatory risk. These professionals can offer tailored advice and insights into how evolving regulations might impact specific investment strategies and suggest adjustments to comply with current and anticipated legal frameworks. Additionally, investing in cryptocurrencies and projects with a clear commitment to compliance and regulatory engagement can further mitigate this risk. Projects that proactively work with regulators and aim for transparency and legal clarity are less likely to face sudden regulatory challenges that could negatively impact their value.

Security Risk

Cybersecurity risk in the realm of cryptocurrency investment encompasses the potential for loss or theft of digital assets due to malicious cyber activities, including hacking, phishing, malware, and other forms of cyberattacks. The digital and decentralized nature of cryptocurrencies makes them inherently vulnerable to such threats. High-profile breaches of cryptocurrency exchanges and wallets have underscored the critical importance of cybersecurity within this space. These incidents not only lead to direct financial losses for investors but also shake confidence in the security of digital assets more broadly, potentially affecting market stability and the value of cryptocurrencies.

The first step in mitigating cybersecurity risk is understanding the common threats faced by cryptocurrency investors. Hacking attempts on exchanges and wallets are among the most direct threats, with attackers often seeking to exploit security vulnerabilities to gain unauthorized access to digital assets. Phishing scams, where attackers deceive individuals into revealing sensitive information such as private keys or login credentials, are also prevalent. Additionally, investors may encounter malware designed to steal cryptocurrencies by infecting devices used to access digital wallets.

To protect against these risks, employing robust security practices is paramount. Using hardware wallets for storing significant amounts of cryptocurrencies provides a higher level of security compared to online wallets, as hardware wallets store private keys offline, making them inaccessible to online hackers. For smaller, more liquid amounts intended for trading, reputable exchanges with strong security measures and insurance policies should be used. Moreover, enabling two-factor authentication (2FA) on all accounts related to cryptocurrency transactions adds an extra layer of security, significantly reducing the risk of unauthorized access.

Beyond individual security measures, diversification plays a crucial role in mitigating cybersecurity risk. By spreading investments across different platforms, technologies, and even asset types, investors can reduce the impact of any single security breach. This approach mirrors the broader principle of investment diversification to manage risk. Additionally, staying informed about the latest cybersecurity threats and protective measures in the cryptocurrency space is crucial. The landscape of cyber threats evolves rapidly, and what constitutes best practice for security today may change tomorrow.

Finally, engaging with communities and platforms that prioritize security can enhance an investor's ability to safeguard their assets. Participating in forums, attending webinars, and following reputable cybersecurity experts on social media can provide valuable insights into current threats and emerging security technologies. Investors who are well-informed about cybersecurity risks and proactive in implementing protective measures are better positioned to secure their digital assets against the ever-present threat of cyberattacks.

Chapter 5: Expected Return on Investment in Cryptocurrencies

Cryptocurrency investments represent a paradigm shift from traditional asset classes, offering unique opportunities and challenges for investors seeking to navigate this digital frontier. This chapter systematically explores the expected Return on Investment (ROI) from cryptocurrencies, dissecting the multifactorial influences, scrutinizing historical market behaviors, and juxtaposing long-term versus short-term investment paradigms.

The allure of cryptocurrencies extends beyond their potential for substantial financial returns; it encapsulates the fusion of technological innovation with financial market evolution. The digital currency ecosystem is marked by its pronounced volatility, the rapid pace of technological advancement, and an emerging regulatory framework. These elements collectively shape the investment landscape, significantly influencing the ROI attainable by market participants. An in-depth understanding of these dynamics is imperative for crafting investment strategies that are resilient, adaptable, and aligned with individual financial objectives and risk profiles.

Factors Influencing ROI in Cryptocurrencies

Market Volatility

The cryptocurrency market's volatility is unparalleled in the financial world, driven by speculative trading, liquidity variations, and sentiment-driven market movements. This section delineates the mechanisms through which volatility impacts ROI, employing statistical measures such as standard deviation and beta coefficients to quantify risk and potential returns.

Adoption and Utility

The intrinsic value and, by extension, the ROI of a cryptocurrency are heavily influenced by its adoption rate and practical utility. This segment explores the correlation between increased adoption of blockchain technology across various sectors and the appreciation in value of cryptocurrencies, supported by case studies and adoption metrics.

Regulatory Environment

Regulatory actions and policies in key jurisdictions can precipitate significant market reactions, affecting cryptocurrency valuations and investor ROI. An analysis of historical regulatory milestones, from the initial laissez-faire approach to recent efforts at establishing comprehensive legal frameworks, provides insights into regulatory risk management.

Technological Developments

Technological innovations within the blockchain domain can catalyze shifts in investment patterns and market valuations. This section examines how advancements such as scalability solutions, interoperability protocols, and consensus mechanism innovations contribute to the speculative and intrinsic value of digital assets.

Historical Performance of Cryptocurrencies

Analysis of Major Cryptocurrencies

A detailed examination of the price history and market cycles of leading cryptocurrencies reveals patterns and trends that can inform future investment decisions. This analysis incorporates quantitative data analysis techniques to chart historical performance trajectories and identify determinants of significant price movements.

Market Trends and Cycles

Understanding the cyclical nature of the cryptocurrency market is crucial for anticipating potential ROI. This part of the chapter applies cycle analysis methodologies to dissect past market phases, offering a framework for predicting future trends based on historical precedents.

Impact of External Factors

External economic, political, and social factors exert a considerable influence on cryptocurrency markets. Through a series of case studies, this section explores the relationship between global events and cryptocurrency valuations, employing econometric models to elucidate these dynamics.

Long-term vs. Short-term Investment Strategies

Long-term Investment Considerations

This section advocates for a strategic perspective on long-term cryptocurrency investments, emphasizing the role of compound interest, market cycle timing, and portfolio diversification in enhancing ROI. It also addresses the psychological and financial discipline required for successful long-term investing.

Short-term Trading Strategies

Contrasting with long-term investment, short-term trading strategies seek to capitalize on market volatility. This segment details approaches such as day trading and swing trading, discussing the analytical tools and risk management techniques essential for navigating short-term market fluctuations.

Strategic Risk Management

Regardless of the investment timeframe, effective risk management is paramount. This final section synthesizes risk mitigation principles, including stop-loss orders, position sizing, and diversification across asset classes, to protect and maximize ROI.

Investing in cryptocurrencies demands a comprehensive grasp of the factors influencing ROI, an appreciation of the market's historical dynamics, and a nuanced approach to investment strategy formulation. By applying the analytical frameworks and methodologies outlined in this chapter, investors can navigate the cryptocurrency landscape with greater confidence and precision, optimizing their potential for return in alignment with their risk tolerance and investment goals.

Chapter 6: Popular Cryptocurrencies

Cryptocurrencies have seen an explosion in popularity over the past decade, with thousands of digital assets now in circulation. In the ever-expanding universe of cryptocurrencies, there are thousands of digital assets vying for attention and investment. However, only a select few have managed to rise to prominence and capture the imagination of investors worldwide. In this chapter, we'll explore some of the most popular cryptocurrencies, examining their features, use cases, and potential for long-term growth.

1. Bitcoin (BTC):

Bitcoin, created by an anonymous individual or group of individuals using the pseudonym Satoshi Nakamoto, is the first and most well-known cryptocurrency. It operates on a decentralized network using blockchain technology, with the primary aim of enabling peer-to-peer transactions without the need for intermediaries. Bitcoin's scarcity, capped at 21 million coins, and its role as a store of value have contributed to its status as digital gold. While Bitcoin's primary use case is as a medium of exchange and store of value, it has also garnered attention as a hedge against inflation and geopolitical uncertainty.

2. Ethereum (ETH):

Ethereum is a decentralized platform that enables the creation of smart contracts and decentralized applications (DApps). Founded by Vitalik Buterin in 2015, Ethereum introduced the concept of programmable money, allowing developers to build decentralized applications and execute self-executing contracts on its blockchain. Ether (ETH) is the native cryptocurrency of the Ethereum network, used to pay for transaction fees and computational services. Ethereum's versatility and programmability have led to its widespread adoption across various industries, including finance, gaming, and supply chain management.

3. Binance Coin (BNB):

Binance Coin is the native cryptocurrency of the Binance exchange, one of the largest cryptocurrency exchanges globally. Initially launched as an ERC-20 token on the Ethereum blockchain, BNB migrated to its blockchain, Binance Smart Chain (BSC), in 2021. BNB serves multiple purposes within the Binance ecosystem, including paying for transaction fees, participating in token sales on the Binance Launchpad, and accessing various DeFi services on Binance Smart Chain. Binance Coin has experienced significant growth in recent years, driven by the expansion of the Binance ecosystem and the growing popularity of decentralized finance (DeFi).

4. Cardano (ADA):

Cardano is a blockchain platform that aims to provide a secure and scalable infrastructure for the development of decentralized applications and smart contracts. Founded by Charles Hoskinson, one of the co-founders of Ethereum, Cardano distinguishes itself through its scientific approach to development and emphasis on peer-reviewed research. ADA is the native cryptocurrency of the Cardano network, used for staking, transaction fees, and governance. Cardano's focus on scalability, interoperability, and sustainability has garnered attention from developers and investors alike, positioning it as a prominent player in the blockchain space.

5. Solana (SOL):

Solana is a high-performance blockchain platform designed for decentralized applications and crypto-native projects. Founded by Anatoly Yakovenko in 2020, Solana aims to address the scalability and throughput limitations of existing blockchain networks by introducing innovative consensus mechanisms and architectural optimizations. SOL is the native cryptocurrency of the Solana network, used for transaction fees, staking, and participation in decentralized governance. Solana's high throughput, low latency, and low transaction costs have positioned it as a leading platform for decentralized finance (DeFi) and non-fungible tokens (NFTs).

6. Polkadot (DOT):

Polkadot is a multi-chain blockchain platform that enables interoperability between different blockchains, allowing them to communicate and share data seamlessly. Founded by Dr. Gavin Wood, one of the co-founders of Ethereum, Polkadot aims to create a decentralized and interoperable web where users have control over their data and digital identities. DOT is the native cryptocurrency of the Polkadot network, used for staking, governance, and bonding. Polkadot's focus on interoperability, scalability, and security has positioned it as a key player in the burgeoning blockchain ecosystem.

7. Ripple (XRP):

Ripple is a digital payment protocol that enables fast, low-cost cross-border transactions. Founded by Chris Larsen and Jed McCaleb in 2012, Ripple aims to revolutionize the global payments industry by providing a more efficient alternative to traditional payment networks like SWIFT. XRP is the native cryptocurrency of the Ripple network, used as a bridge currency for facilitating cross-border transactions and liquidity provision. Ripple's partnerships with financial institutions and focus on regulatory compliance have positioned it as a leading player in the realm of enterprise blockchain solutions.

8. Dogecoin (DOGE):

Dogecoin started as a joke cryptocurrency based on the popular "Doge" meme but has since evolved into a legitimate digital asset with a vibrant community and widespread adoptionFounded by Billy Markus and Jackson Palmer in 2013, Dogecoin aims to be a fun and accessible cryptocurrency that appeals to a broad audience. DOGE is known for its active community, philanthropic initiatives, and meme-centric culture. While Dogecoin's utility as a payment method is limited compared to other cryptocurrencies, it remains popular among retail investors and social media enthusiasts.

9. Litecoin (LTC):

Litecoin is a peer-to-peer cryptocurrency created by Charlie Lee in 2011, serving as a "lite" version of Bitcoin. Litecoin aims to provide faster transaction times and lower fees compared to Bitcoin, making it suitable for everyday transactions and micropayments. LTC is often referred to as the "silver to Bitcoin's gold" due to its similarities to Bitcoin in terms of technology and scarcity. Litecoin's adoption as a payment method and store of value has grown steadily over the years, making it one of the oldest and most established cryptocurrencies in the market.

10. Chainlink (LINK):

Chainlink is a decentralized oracle network that connects smart contracts with real-world data, enabling them to interact with external systems and access off-chain information. Founded by Sergey Nazarov and Steve Ellis in 2017, Chainlink aims to solve the "oracle problem" by providing reliable and tamper-proof data feeds to smart contracts. LINK is the native cryptocurrency of the Chainlink network, used for paying node operators and accessing data feeds. Chainlink's role in bridging the gap between blockchain and real-world data has positioned it as a critical infrastructure component for the decentralized web.

The cryptocurrency market is home to a diverse array of digital assets, each with its unique features, use cases, and potential for investment. While Bitcoin remains the most prominent and widely recognized cryptocurrency, there are numerous other projects and platforms vying for attention and adoption. By conducting thorough research, assessing the fundamentals, and understanding the market dynamics, investors can identify promising cryptocurrencies and capitalize on their potential for long-term growth and value creation.

Chapter 7: How to Invest in Cryptocurrencies

The ascent of cryptocurrency from a niche digital asset to a mainstream financial instrument has captivated investors globally. As the digital currency landscape expands, it's marked by the introduction of thousands of cryptocurrencies, each offering unique value propositions and investment opportunities. This surge in interest has necessitated a comprehensive guide for newcomers and seasoned investors alike, aiming to navigate the complexities of cryptocurrency investments effectively. This chapter serves as a foundational primer, delineating the pivotal steps in commencing your investment journey, from the initial selection of a cryptocurrency exchange to the intricate process of managing digital wallets, and culminating in the strategic acquisition and divestment of digital assets. Through a detailed exploration of these critical stages, investors are equipped with the knowledge to make informed decisions, optimize their investment strategies, and navigate the volatile waters of the cryptocurrency market with confidence and insight.

The transformative journey of investing in cryptocurrencies is not just about tapping into a new asset class; it's about participating in the evolution of global finance. The allure of digital currencies lies in their potential to redefine economic paradigms, offering unparalleled opportunities for growth, diversification, and innovation. As we delve into the mechanics of investing in this digital realm, it's crucial to approach with a blend of enthusiasm and caution. Understanding the foundational elements of cryptocurrency investments, such as exchanges, wallets, and investment strategies, is the first step toward leveraging the potential of this dynamic market. This chapter aims to empower you with the essential knowledge and tools to navigate the cryptocurrency landscape effectively, making informed decisions that align with your financial goals and risk tolerance.

Choosing a Cryptocurrency Exchange

Choosing the right cryptocurrency exchange is a critical first step for any investor entering the digital currency market. Exchanges vary widely in terms of security features, fees, user interface, and the range of cryptocurrencies offered. Some of the most popular exchanges include Coinbase, known for its user-friendly interface and robust security measures; Binance, celebrated for its extensive selection of cryptocurrencies and low trading fees; and Kraken, which offers a comprehensive suite of trading tools and strong regulatory compliance. Each exchange has its unique advantages, catering to different investor needs and preferences.

When selecting an exchange, investors should consider the platform's security protocols, such as two-factor authentication, cold storage options, and insurance policies against theft or hacking incidents. Fee structures are also an important consideration, as they can vary significantly between exchanges and impact overall investment returns. Additionally, the availability of specific cryptocurrencies and trading pairs, as well as the exchange's geographic restrictions, should align with the investor's goals and location.

Ultimately, the choice of exchange should be informed by thorough research and consideration of personal investment strategies. It's advisable to review and compare the features, fees, security measures, and user reviews of multiple exchanges. This careful selection process ensures investors find a platform that not only meets their immediate trading needs but also supports their long-term investment objectives in the ever-evolving cryptocurrency market.

Setting Up a Digital Wallet: A Comprehensive Guide

When embarking on your cryptocurrency investment journey, establishing a digital wallet is a foundational step. The digital wallet landscape offers a spectrum of options tailored to diverse needs, encompassing hardware wallets renowned for their robust security, software wallets lauded for user-friendly interfaces, and mobile wallets prized for their accessibility. This variety ensures that investors can choose a wallet type that best suits their security requirements and lifestyle preferences.

Security in the realm of digital wallets cannot be overstressed. Investors are advised to adhere to stringent security protocols, including the meticulous management of private keys and recovery phrases, which are the linchpins of wallet security. These measures are critical in thwarting unauthorized access and safeguarding digital assets against the ever-present threats of hacking and cyber theft.

Navigating the setup of a digital wallet involves a series of calculated steps, starting with the selection of a wallet that aligns with your security needs and investment intentions. Following this, the process extends to implementing security measures designed to shield your digital assets from potential cyber threats. This careful approach to setting up and securing a digital wallet lays the groundwork for a secure and efficient cryptocurrency investment experience.

Strategies for Buying and Selling Cryptocurrencies

Developing effective strategies for buying and selling cryptocurrencies involves understanding market analysis techniques. Technical analysis and fundamental analysis are key methods used to gauge market sentiment, value, and potential future movements of digital currencies. Investors rely on these analyses to make informed decisions, timing their trades based on market trends and indicators.

Investment strategies in the cryptocurrency domain vary widely, from long-term holding, known as "HODLing," to more active approaches like day trading and swing trading. Each strategy carries its own set of risks and rewards, influenced by market volatility and investor's risk tolerance. Long-term investors often focus on the fundamental value and potential of a cryptocurrency, while traders might exploit short-term market fluctuations for profit.

Risk management is crucial in the volatile world of cryptocurrency investing. Diversification, setting stop-loss orders, and only investing what one can afford to lose are prudent practices. These strategies help mitigate the impact of market volatility, protecting the investor's portfolio from significant losses. Effective risk management supports sustained participation in the market, enabling investors to capitalize on opportunities while minimizing potential downsides.

Chapter 8: Secure Investment Practices

In the dynamic realm of cryptocurrency investment, understanding and implementing secure investment practices is not just advantageous—it's imperative. As investors venture into the volatile world of digital currencies, the significance of protecting their assets against a backdrop of cyber threats and scams becomes paramount. This chapter aims to unravel the complexities of cryptocurrency security, offering insights into the judicious selection of storage options and the adoption of rigorous security measures.

The journey toward secure cryptocurrency investment is fraught with challenges, yet it offers the informed investor a path to safeguard their assets effectively. By highlighting the critical steps for robust asset protection, including the nuances of digital wallet security and strategies to evade common digital pitfalls, this introduction sets the stage for a deeper exploration of secure investment practices. Our goal is to equip readers with the knowledge and tools necessary to navigate the cryptocurrency market safely, ensuring their investments are well-protected in an ever-evolving digital landscape.

The realm of cryptocurrency storage is vast, featuring cold storage, hardware, software, and paper wallets, each with unique benefits and drawbacks. Cold storage and hardware wallets offer heightened security by keeping assets offline, ideal for long-term investors seeking to minimize exposure to cyber threats. Software wallets, accessible and convenient, suit those engaging in frequent transactions, despite their vulnerability to online risks. Paper wallets, though secure, require meticulous physical safeguarding, making them a fit for investors comfortable with offline, physical storage solutions. Each type caters to different investor needs, balancing security with convenience.

Multi-signature wallets enhance security for organizations and investment groups by requiring multiple approvals for transactions, mitigating the risk of unauthorized access. For institutional investors, custody solutions offer a secure way to hold digital assets, incorporating regulatory compliance and insurance to protect investments. These advanced storage solutions provide a robust framework for managing and safeguarding large-scale cryptocurrency portfolios, addressing the specific needs and regulatory requirements of professional investors.

Adopting best practices for crypto asset security is crucial, emphasizing the use of strong, unique passwords. Utilizing password management tools can aid in generating and storing complex passwords, enhancing account security. Equally important is keeping software, including wallets and security applications, up to date. Regular updates ensure the latest security enhancements and vulnerability fixes are applied, safeguarding against potential cyber threats. This holistic approach to security, combining robust password policies with diligent software maintenance, forms a critical defense layer for protecting digital assets.

Two-Factor Authentication (2FA) significantly enhances crypto security by adding an extra verification step. SMS, app-based authenticators, and hardware tokens are common 2FA methods, each providing a different level of security and convenience. SMS offers ease of use, while app-based solutions like Google Authenticator or Authy provide better security. Hardware tokens, considered the most secure, generate codes offline. Emerging technologies, such as biometric verification and decentralized identity verification, promise to further bolster crypto security by leveraging unique personal attributes or blockchain-based solutions, enhancing protection against unauthorized access.

Operational security in the realm of cryptocurrency extends beyond technical safeguards to encompass the human element, underscoring the necessity for comprehensive training and awareness. Recognizing phishing attempts and social engineering tactics becomes paramount, as these methods exploit human vulnerabilities rather than technological loopholes. By fostering a culture of vigilance and educating users on the hallmarks of such schemes, individuals can significantly mitigate the risk of compromising their digital assets.

Additionally, adopting safe browsing habits and utilizing Virtual Private Networks (VPNs) can further enhance online privacy and security. VPNs encrypt internet traffic, shielding it from interception or monitoring, thereby protecting sensitive information from potential eavesdroppers. Coupled with safe browsing practices, such as avoiding suspicious links and regularly updating browser software, these measures form a robust defense against the array of threats targeting crypto investors today.

Conducting regular security audits of personal crypto holdings and associated accounts is essential for maintaining asset security. This process involves reviewing wallet access protocols, transaction histories, and the security of exchange platforms used. Utilizing tools and services designed for blockchain analysis and wallet security can greatly aid in this process. These tools help identify potential vulnerabilities and unauthorized transactions. Interpreting their findings requires a focus on discrepancies in transaction patterns and unauthorized access attempts, ensuring swift action can be taken to secure assets effectively.

Identifying and avoiding scams in the cryptocurrency world is crucial. Common scams include Ponzi schemes, phishing websites, and fraudulent Initial Coin Offerings (ICOs). Scammers often use psychological tactics such as offering guaranteed returns or creating a sense of urgency to exploit potential victims. To critically evaluate investment opportunities, it's important to research extensively, verify the credibility of the project or platform, and be wary of offers that seem too good to be true. Understanding these scams and the strategies used can help investors navigate investments more safely.

The crypto community plays a pivotal role in identifying and sharing information about scams, creating an environment of mutual support and vigilance. Through forums and social media platforms, investors can report suspicious activities, sharing their experiences to warn others. Regulatory bodies and dedicated platforms also offer channels for reporting scams, aiding in fraud prevention efforts. Active participation in these community networks not only empowers individuals but also contributes to a safer investment landscape for everyone involved in the cryptocurrency space.

Adhering to secure investment practices is paramount in safeguarding assets and fostering a positive cryptocurrency market experience. As the landscape continually evolves, it's crucial to engage in ongoing education and remain vigilant. This proactive approach not only protects individual investments but also contributes to the overall health and integrity of the crypto ecosystem.

In wrapping up Chapter 8, we highlight the indispensable role of security in cryptocurrency investing. From choosing secure storage methods to navigating scams, the chapter lays out a comprehensive roadmap for safeguarding digital assets. It stresses the importance of continuous learning and community collaboration in adapting to new threats. The evolving digital landscape demands vigilance and proactive measures to ensure a secure and positive investment experience in the dynamic world of cryptocurrency.

Chapter 9: Resources for American Investors

In the fast-paced world of cryptocurrency investing, having access to reliable resources is essential for making informed decisions and navigating the complexities of the market. In this chapter, we will explore various resources tailored specifically for American investors, ranging from cryptocurrency exchanges to trusted sources for market analysis and regulatory guidance.

Recommended Cryptocurrency Exchanges

Choosing the right cryptocurrency exchange is crucial for executing trades efficiently and securely. For American investors, several reputable exchanges cater to their specific needs, offering a wide range of cryptocurrencies, robust security measures, and compliance with regulatory requirements.

Coinbase:

Coinbase is one of the most popular cryptocurrency exchanges in the United States, known for its user-friendly interface, extensive coin offerings, and strong regulatory compliance. The platform provides a seamless onboarding experience for beginners and advanced trading features for seasoned investors. Additionally, Coinbase offers a secure wallet solution for storing cryptocurrencies and a user-friendly mobile app for trading on the go.

Kraken:

Kraken is another well-established cryptocurrency exchange that caters to American investors. With a strong focus on security and regulatory compliance, Kraken offers a diverse selection of cryptocurrencies, advanced trading tools, and competitive fees. The platform is renowned for its robust security features, including cold storage for the majority of user funds and two-factor authentication for account protection.
Binance.US:

Binance.US is the American arm of the global cryptocurrency exchange Binance, offering a tailored experience for US-based traders. The platform provides a wide range of cryptocurrencies for trading, competitive fees, and advanced trading features such as margin trading and futures contracts. Binance.US prioritizes regulatory compliance and has obtained licenses to operate in various states across the country.

These are just a few examples of cryptocurrency exchanges available to American investors. It's essential to conduct thorough research and due diligence before choosing an exchange, considering factors such as security measures, supported cryptocurrencies, trading fees, and user experience.

Trusted Sources for Market Analysis and Research

In the dynamic and rapidly evolving cryptocurrency market, staying informed about market trends, news, and developments is paramount for making informed investment decisions. Fortunately, there are several trusted sources of market analysis and research tailored specifically for American investors.

CoinDesk:

CoinDesk is a leading cryptocurrency news and media platform that provides in-depth analysis, market insights, and breaking news coverage. With a team of seasoned journalists and industry experts, CoinDesk offers comprehensive coverage of the cryptocurrency market, regulatory developments, and emerging trends. Additionally, CoinDesk hosts industry events and conferences, bringing together thought leaders and stakeholders from across the globe.

CryptoSlate:

CryptoSlate is a popular cryptocurrency media outlet that offers a wide range of resources for investors, including news, analysis, research reports, and educational content. The platform provides real-time data on cryptocurrencies, blockchain projects, and market trends, helping investors stay ahead of the curve. Additionally, CryptoSlate features comprehensive ICO and token sale listings, allowing investors to discover and participate in promising blockchain projects.

The Block:

The Block is a respected cryptocurrency research and analysis firm that provides institutional-grade insights and intelligence to investors, traders, and industry professionals. The firm offers a range of subscription-based products, including research reports, market analysis, and data analytics tools, tailored to the needs of institutional investors. With a focus on transparency and integrity, The Block is trusted by leading financial institutions and cryptocurrency firms worldwide.

These are just a few examples of trusted sources for market analysis and research available to American investors. It's essential to diversify information sources and cross-reference data to ensure accuracy and reliability.

Regulatory Bodies and Legal Resources

Navigating the regulatory landscape is a critical aspect of cryptocurrency investing, particularly for American investors who must comply with federal and state regulations. Understanding the role of regulatory bodies and accessing reliable legal resources is essential for ensuring compliance and mitigating regulatory risk.

U.S. Securities and Exchange Commission (SEC):

The U.S. Securities and Exchange Commission (SEC) is the primary regulatory agency responsible for overseeing securities markets and enforcing federal securities laws. The SEC plays a crucial role in regulating the cryptocurrency industry, particularly with regard to initial coin offerings (ICOs), securities exchanges, and investment products. American investors can access valuable information and guidance on cryptocurrency regulations through the SEC's website, including enforcement actions, investor alerts, and regulatory updates.

Commodity Futures Trading Commission (CFTC):

The Commodity Futures Trading Commission (CFTC) is another key regulatory agency that oversees derivatives markets and protects investors from fraud and manipulation. The CFTC has jurisdiction over cryptocurrency derivatives such as futures contracts and options, ensuring fair and transparent trading practices. American investors can find useful resources and educational materials on cryptocurrency derivatives on the CFTC's website, including regulatory guidance and enforcement actions.

Financial Industry Regulatory Authority (FINRA):

The Financial Industry Regulatory Authority (FINRA) is a self-regulatory organization that oversees brokerage firms and registered representatives operating in the United States. While FINRA does not directly regulate cryptocurrencies, it provides investor education and resources on emerging investment products and scams, including cryptocurrencies and digital assets. American investors can access FINRA's website for educational materials, investor alerts, and tools to check the background of brokers and investment professionals.

In addition to regulatory bodies, American investors can seek guidance from legal experts specializing in cryptocurrency law and regulation. Engaging with experienced legal counsel can help investors navigate complex legal issues, ensure compliance with regulatory requirements, and protect their interests in the cryptocurrency market.

In conclusion, American investors have access to a wide range of resources tailored specifically for navigating the cryptocurrency market, including reputable exchanges, trusted sources for market analysis and research, and regulatory bodies providing guidance on compliance and legal requirements. By leveraging these resources effectively, investors can make informed decisions, mitigate risks, and capitalize on opportunities in the dynamic world of cryptocurrencies.

Chapter 10: Conclusion and Next Steps

As we conclude our journey through the intricate world of cryptocurrency investment, it's essential to reflect on key insights gleaned from our exploration and chart a course for the future. In this final chapter, we'll recap the essential points covered in this guide, outline actionable steps for getting started with cryptocurrency investment, and offer a glimpse into the future outlook for the cryptocurrency market.

Recap of Key Points

Throughout this guide, we've delved into various aspects of cryptocurrency investment, from understanding the fundamentals of cryptocurrencies to assessing investment risks and exploring resources for American investors. Here's a brief recap of the key points covered:

- **Understanding Cryptocurrencies:** We started by defining cryptocurrencies and exploring their brief history, highlighting their decentralized nature and transformative potential.

- **Investment Considerations:** We discussed the reasons for investing in cryptocurrencies, including their potential for high returns, portfolio diversification benefits, and hedge against inflation.

- **Market Dynamics and Volatility:** We examined the market dynamics and volatility inherent in the cryptocurrency market, emphasizing the importance of risk management strategies to navigate market fluctuations effectively.

- **Assessing Investment Risks:** We explored various investment risks, including market risk, inflation risk, regulatory risk, and security risk, and discussed proactive measures to mitigate these risks.

- **Resources for American Investors:** We identified recommended cryptocurrency exchanges, trusted sources for market analysis and research, and regulatory bodies providing guidance on compliance and legal requirements for American investors.

Actionable Steps for Getting Started with Cryptocurrency Investment

Now that we've covered the fundamentals and key considerations, let's outline actionable steps for getting started with cryptocurrency investment:

- **Educate Yourself:** Continuously educate yourself about cryptocurrencies, blockchain technology, and investment strategies through reputable sources, books, courses, and industry events.

- **Set Investment Goals:** Define your investment goals, risk tolerance, and time horizon to tailor your investment strategy to your unique financial objectives.

- **Diversify Your Portfolio:** Diversify your cryptocurrency portfolio by investing in a mix of established cryptocurrencies, promising altcoins, and other asset classes to mitigate risk and maximize potential returns.

- **Choose a Secure Exchange:** Select a reputable and secure cryptocurrency exchange that aligns with your trading needs, regulatory compliance requirements, and security standards.

- **Implement Risk Management:** Implement robust risk management strategies, including setting stop-loss orders, diversifying investments, and staying informed about market developments and trends.

- **Stay Informed:** Stay abreast of market news, regulatory updates, and technological advancements in the cryptocurrency space to make informed investment decisions and adapt your strategy accordingly.

Future Outlook for the Cryptocurrency Market

Looking ahead, the future of the cryptocurrency market appears promising, driven by continued adoption, technological innovation, and institutional involvement. While challenges and uncertainties remain, including regulatory developments and market volatility, the long-term trajectory of cryptocurrencies remains upward.

Institutional interest in cryptocurrencies is growing, with major financial institutions, corporations, and asset managers increasingly allocating capital to digital assets. Additionally, advancements in blockchain technology, such as scalability solutions and interoperability protocols, are paving the way for broader adoption and use cases beyond speculative trading.

Furthermore, the integration of cryptocurrencies into traditional financial systems and the emergence of central bank digital currencies (CBDCs) are reshaping the global monetary landscape, offering new opportunities and challenges for investors and policymakers alike.

In conclusion, the cryptocurrency market represents a dynamic and evolving ecosystem with significant growth potential and opportunities for investors. By understanding the fundamentals, mitigating risks, and staying informed, investors can navigate the cryptocurrency market with confidence and position themselves for success in the digital economy of the future.